Poems about
Journeys

Selected by
Amanda Earl & Danielle Sensier

Illustrated by
Frances Lloyd

Wayland

Titles in the series
Poems about . . .

Animals	**Food**
Colours	**Homes**
Families	**Journeys**
Feelings	**Weather**

For Christopher

Series editor: Catherine Baxter
Designer: Loraine Hayes

First published in 1994 by
Wayland (Publishers) Ltd
61 Western Road, Hove
East Sussex BN3 1JD, England

© Copyright 1994 Wayland
(Publishers) Ltd

British Library Cataloguing in Publication Data

Poems About Journeys. – (Poems About . . .
Series)
 I. Earl, Amanda II. Sensier, Danielle
 III. Series
 808.81

ISBN 0-7502-1036-2

Front cover: Girl in go-cart/design S. Balley

Typeset by Dorchester Typesetting
Group Ltd., Dorset, England.
Printed and bound in Italy by
G. Canale & C.S.p.A., Turin.

Poets' nationalities

David McCord	English
Judith Nicholls	English
Tac Lang Pee	Chinese
Phyllis McGinley	American
Clive Sansom	English
Robert Louis Stevenson	Scottish
Christina Rossetti	English/Italian
Danielle Sensier	English
Jeff Moss	American
Michael Rosen	English
Rabindranath Tagore	Indian
Matsuo Basho	Japanese

Contents

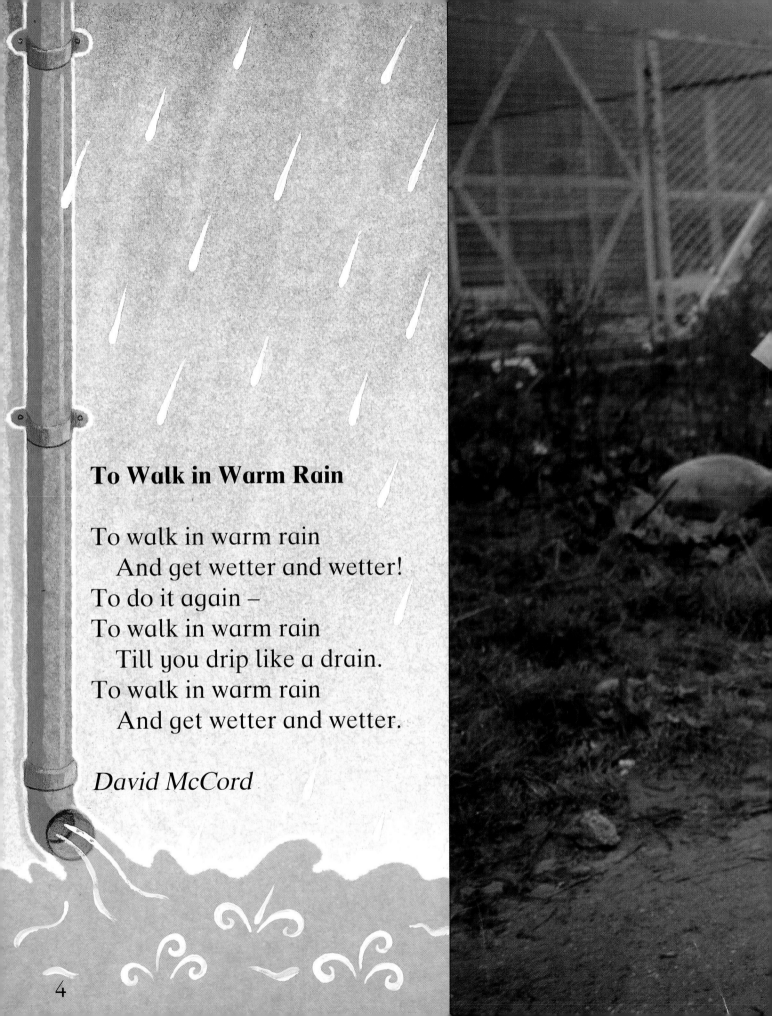

To Walk in Warm Rain

To walk in warm rain
    And get wetter and wetter!
To do it again –
To walk in warm rain
    Till you drip like a drain.
To walk in warm rain
    And get wetter and wetter.

David McCord

The mountain

It was my birthday
I was six
my dad and I
climbed to the top
of the mountain
The car looked tiny
   Dad wanted to give up
   I didn't

When we got to the top
I said 'yippee'
Then we climbed
back down.

Thomas Lloyd
(aged 6)

6

Biking

Fingers grip,
toes curl;
head down,
wheels whirl.

Hair streams,
fields race;
ears sting,
winds chase.

Breathe deep,
troubles gone;
just feel
windsong.

Judith Nicholls

Hill rolling

I kind of exploded inside,
and joy shot out of me.
I began to roll down the grassy hill
I bent my knees up small, took a deep breath
and I was off.
My arms shot out sideways.
I gathered speed.
My eyes squinted
Sky and grass, dazzle and dark.
I went on forever,
My arms were covered with dents,
holes, squashed grass.
Before I knew it I was at the bottom.
The game was over.

*Andrew Taylor
(aged 10)*

All Aboard!

Hurry, scurry, in the car!
Push that dog down, lock the door!
Where's my bucket? In the boot;
move that deckchair off my foot!

Are we in now? Wait a minute,
here's a shoe with no one in it!
Bats and buckets, spades and balls,
plastic macs for sudden squalls* . . .

Hurry, scurry: lock the door!
Get that dog down on the floor!
Hurry, scurry: wait for me!
Who'll be first to see the sea?

Food and chairs and picnic bag,
Grandpa, Sue, the boys, the dog:
Mum with maps and sandwich box,
Dad white-legged in winter socks . . .

Hurry, scurry: lock that door –
this poor car will take no more!
Hurry, scurry; turn the key,
We're off at last to see the sea!

Judith Nicholls

* small storms

Sampan

Waves lap lap
Fish fins clap clap
Brown sails flap flap
Chop-sticks tap tap
Up and down the long green river
Ohe Ohe lanterns quiver
Willow branches brush the river
Ohe Ohe lanterns quiver
Waves lap lap
Fish fins clap clap
Brown sails flap flap
Chop-sticks tap tap

Tac Lang Pee

We're Racing, Racing down the Walk

We're racing, racing down the walk
Over the pavement and round the block.
We rumble along till the sidewalk ends –
Felicia and I and half our friends.
Our hair flies backward. It's whish and whirr!
She roars at me and I shout at her
As past the porches and garden gates
We rattle and rock
On our roller skates.

Phyllis McGinley

Funny the way different cars start

Funny the way
Different cars start.
Some with a chunk and a jerk,
Some with a cough and a puff of smoke
Out of the back,
some with only a little click –
                with hardly a noise.

Funny the way
Different cars run.
Some rattle and bang,
Some whirr,
Some knock and knock.
Some purr
and hummmmm
Smoothly on
                with hardly any noise.

Dorothy Baruch

Twinkle Twinkle Chocolate Bar

Twinkle twinkle chocolate bar
My dad drives a rusty car
Press the starter
Pull the choke
Off he goes in a cloud of smoke.

Anonymous

The Engine Driver

The train goes running along the line,
Jicketty-can.
I wish it were mine, I wish it were mine,
Jicketty-can, jicketty-can.
The engine driver stands in front,
He makes it run, he makes it shunt;

Out of the town,
Out of the town,
Over the hill,
Over the down,
Under the bridges,
Across the lea,
Over the ridge
And down to the sea,
With a jicketty-can, jicketty-can,
Jicketty-jicketty-jicketty-can,
Jicketty-can, jicketty-can.

Clive Sansom

There was a young lady from Spain
Who was dreadfully sick on a train,
Not once – but again
and again and again
and again and again and again.

Anonymous

Windy Nights

Whenever the moon and stars are set,
   Whenever the wind is high,
All night long in the dark and wet,
   A man goes riding by.
Late in the night when the fires are out,
Why does he gallop and gallop about?

Whenever the trees are crying aloud,
   And ships are tossed at sea,
By, on the highway, low and loud,
   By at the gallop goes he.
By at the gallop he goes, and then
By he comes back at the gallop again.

Robert Louis Stevenson

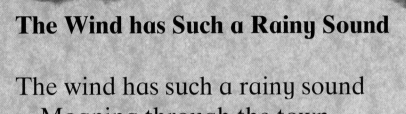

The Wind has Such a Rainy Sound

The wind has such a rainy sound
   Moaning through the town,
The sea has such a windy sound, –
   Will the ships go down?

The apples in the orchard
   Tumble from their tree. –
Oh, will the ships go down, go down,
   In the windy sea?

Christina Rossetti

Protect me, O Lord;
My boat is so small,
And your sea is so big.

Old Breton Prayer

That sinking feeling

He rocked the boat,
Did Ezra Shank;
These bubbles mark

O
O
O
O
O
O
O
O
O
O
O
O
O
O
O
O

Where Ezra sank.

Anonymous

Round town

At the bus stop in the rain,
been round town and
back again.

Hear the engine
then the bus comes
splashing red into the gloom.

Now it's panic time for feet,
on-and-off
will there be room?

Inside:
damp umbrellas dripping,
shopping bags piled up on legs.

Steamy windows stop me seeing
till my fingers clear the fog.

Outside:
people walking backwards
in a stop-go stop-go world.

Round the corner journey's over,
out through opening-closing doors.

At the bus stop in the rain,
been round town
and home again.

Danielle Sensier

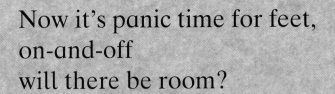

Elevator, Escalator

Elevator*, escalator, subway, bus,
Travelling through the city can be lots of fuss.
It can get a bit confusing for chickens like us,
Elevator, escalator, subway, bus.

Take the elevator up, take the escalator down,
Then a bus through the streets and a subway underground.
Back home on the farm, it's not hard to get around
But the city's complicated when you're downtown.

Oh elevator, escalator, subway, bus,
Travelling through the city can be a lot of fuss.
It can get a bit confusing for chickens like us,
Elevator, escalator, subway, bus.

Jeff Moss

* lift

Gone

She sat in the back of the van   we ran faster
and we waved to her there   she reached out for us

we ran towards her   the van moved faster
but the van moved off   we reached for her hand

she stretched out of the back of the van
we ran, reaching

the van got away
we stopped running

we never reached her
before she was gone.

Michael Rosen

From **Paper Boats**

Day by day I float my paper boats one by one down the running stream.

In big black letters I write my name on them and the name of the village where I live.

I hope that someone in some strange land will find them and know who I am.

I load my little boats with shiuli flowers from our garden, and hope that these blooms of the dawn will be carried safely to land in the night.

Rabindranath Tagore

At Kisagata

At Kisagata
A cherry tree is covered
At times by the waves:
Fishermen must row their boats
Above the cherry blossom.

Matsuo Basho

How to use this book

Poetry is a very enjoyable area of literature and children
take to it naturally, usually beginning with nursery rhymes.
It's what happens next that can make all the difference!
This series of thematic poetry anthologies keeps poetry
alive and enjoyable for young children.

When using these books there are several ways in which
you can help a child to appreciate poetry and to understand
the ways in which words can be carefully chosen and
sculpted to convey different atmospheres and meanings.
Try to encourage the following:

- Joining in when the poem is read out loud.
- Talking about favourite words, phrases or images.
- Discussing the illustration and photographs.
- Miming facial expressions to suit the mood of the poems.
- Acting out events in the poems.
- Copying out the words.
- Learning favourite poems by heart.
- Discussing the difference between a poem and a story.
- Clapping hands to rhythmic poems.
- Talking about metaphors/similes eg what kind of weather
  would a lion be? What colour would sadness be? What
  would it taste like? If you could hold it, how would it
  feel?

It is inevitable that, at some point, children will want to
write poems themselves. Writing a poem is, however, only
one way of enjoying poetry. With the above activities,
children can be encouraged to appreciate and delight in
this unique form of communication.

Picture acknowledgements

APM Studios cover; Collections 27 (Geoff Howard); Life File 6 (Eric Poppke), 7 (Phil Jones), 19 (Ron Bonser); Impact 22 and 23 (Steve Benbow), Still Pictures 4 and 5 (Mark Edwards); Tony Stone Worldwide 9 (Alan Levenson), 14 (Bob Torrez), Zefa 12, 29 (Sander).

Text acknowledgements

For permission to reprint copyright material the publishers gratefully acknowledge the following: Curtis Brown Ltd for 'We're Racing, Racing down the Walk' by Phyllis McGinley from *Sugar and Spice – The ABC of Being a Girl.* Reprinted by permission of Curtis Brown Ltd. Copyright © 1959–1960 Phyllis McGinley; Faber & Faber Limited for 'Biking' from *Midnight Forest and Other Poems* by Judith Nicholls; David Higham Associates for 'The Engine Driver' by Clive Sansom; International Creative Management, Inc for 'Elevator Escalator' by Jeff Moss. © Copyright 1991 Jeff Moss. Reprinted by permission of International Creative Management Inc; Little, Brown & Company for 'To Walk in Warm Rain' by David McCord. Copyright © 1979–1980 David McCord. Reprinted by permission of Little, Brown & Company; The National Exhibition of Children's Art for 'The Mountain' by Thomas Lloyd; Oxford University Press for 'All Aboard' from *Wish You Were Here.* Copyright © 1992 Judith Nicholls. Reprinted by permission of Oxford University Press; Danielle Sensier for 'Round Town'; Scholastic Publications Ltd for 'Gone' from *Don't Put Mustard in the Custard* by Michael Rosen. While every effort has been made to secure permission, in some cases it has proved impossible to trace the copyright holders. The publishers apologise for this apparent negligence.

Index of first lines